Praise for *The Homeowner's Guide to Greatness*:

"If we hadn't read this book, we never would have gotten through the first year in our home. We now keep a copy in every room, just in case."
                    -New Homeowners

"Thanks to *THGG*, we have become home-owning legends in our own time."
                            -Gold medalists in the Home-owning
                            Olympics, an event they were
                            inspired to organize after reading this
                            guide

"I was flattered that I was referenced not once but twice in these helpful pages. I've been living in the shed in my parents backyard for 33 years, but now I think I'm finally ready to make a go of it on my own. Thanks *THGG*."
                    -Pig Pen from the Peanuts Gang

"Buying a house was a drop in the bucket for me, I hire out all menial tasks, and I don't even know what a lawnmower looks like, but I enjoyed reading this book anyway."
                    - An extremely wealthy individual

# THE HOMEOWNER'S GUIDE TO GREATNESS

How to handle natural disasters, design dilemmas,
and various infestations like a champ.

JOCELYN JANE COX

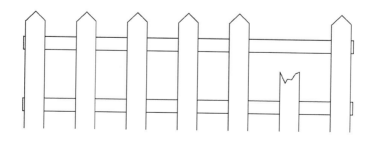

ISBN 978-0-9855287-0-6
Printed in the United States of America

Cover and Book design by Rob Strati

Jocelyn Jane Cox
Visit: www.homeownersguidetogreatness.com

First Printing: April 2012

# Contents

# THE HOMEOWNER'S GUIDE TO GREATNESS

# Introduction

Congratulations! Either you own a house or you are considering buying one. Double congratulations on distinguishing yourself from others in this situation by reading these pages. Just by holding this groundbreaking guide in your hands you are demonstrating that you have what it takes…namely, you have the *desire* to be a great homeowner.

Along this journey, you will have to channel this desire into an infinite number of specific tasks, some of them more challenging than others. You may have to crawl on your roof at the risk of severe bodily harm. You might share your bed pillow with a mouse. You may find yourself sopping up a flooded basement with ultra-absorbent diapers. But before you tackle any of these projects or deal with any unexpected emergencies, you will have to first engage in an activity not usually associated with home ownership: laughter. After all, this is the only surefire way to keep from crying when you and your home are on the cusp of ruin. For example, how are you going to rebuild that wall you accidentally knocked down if you have tears clouding your eyes?

What you will find in the following pages is a wealth of advice based on a bit of experience. A few years ago, my husband and I moved from a loft-style apartment in the South Bronx to a house in the 'burbs with a yard near Nyack, New York. What we have learned is that, owning a home is a cinch as long as you have a good sense of humor (or, alternatively, mountains of money).

If you are about to purchase a house, if you just bought one, or if you have been gradually weighed down by the pressures of maintaining your crumbling property for many years now, this book is guaranteed to help you.

So put on some gardening gloves, a hard hat, a frilly apron…and read on.

# 1. BUYING A HOME

Buying a house is probably one of the most exciting and terrifying experiences most of us will voluntarily undertake. It's kind of like jumping off a cliff, except instead of a parachute, you have a roof. It's not the most logical thing to do, you don't know exactly what's going to happen, and once you jump, it's not an easy process to reverse. But don't despair, if your roof/parachute turns out to have a big hole in it, there are surely some good roofers nearby. Just be sure to get three estimates for the purposes of comparison and scream at the top of your lungs.

# Buying vs. Renting

"To buy or not to buy?" This can be a difficult decision. Most people in this country consider buying a home the ultimate fulfillment of the American Dream and the responsible thing to do. Others see home ownership as a prison, a needless way to be tied down both physically and financially. But what about those of us who vacillate, who want to put their stake in the ground, prove they are upstanding citizens, yet who also dare to ask the scandalous question, "Is it really so bad to rent for the rest of our lives?" This is a very tricky game of ping pong. (Note: ping pong table sold separately.)

What makes this dilemma even more interesting is that you can keep playing it even after you purchase a house (in the form of buyer's remorse) and of course, also after you decide to rent indefinitely (because looking at new home listings is a hard habit to break).

Here are some things to keep in mind:

• RENTING: Yes, paying rent every month is *exactly* like flushing money down the toilet. The only good thing is that if it gets stuck, someone else pays the plumber to plunge it. BUYING: If you have ever used one of those mortgage calculators, available on many internet sites, you will discover that the interest on most 30 year loans makes your house cost at least twice as much in the long run. In fact, you'll probably be paying only the interest on your loan for a long time before ever making a dent in the principle. Basically, buying a house really only makes financial sense if you can buy it out-right, in full, i.e. without taking out a loan. Only two people in this country can actually afford to do this: one of them is named Mark Zuckerberg and the other just bought a tent.

• RENTING: People say that when you pay rent, you end up with nothing to show for it – this is not true: in fact, for however many months or years you have rented, you have enjoyed a special and very tangible thing called shelter. You have had a place to rest your weary head, cupboards to store your favorite belongings, and a hallway to pace while wondering if you'd be a more complete person if you owned your own property. BUYING: On the other hand, you might be interested to know that the word "mortgage" is derived from the Latin *mortuus*, meaning, "to die."

• RENTING: As a renter, you are usually required to pay a chunk of money up front – first month's rent, last month's, and a security deposit. Writing this check is always a painful endeavor. BUYING: But that check is a pleasure in comparison to writing one for closing fees. Of course, these fees compensate the real estate agents, the lawyers, and the title company, all of whom play a critical role in the biggest purchase of your life. You are definitely grateful: so why do you hear the unmistakable sound of a toilet flushing while you hand over the check? (Beware of clogging – see first entry, above.)

• RENTING: Two pesky words renters never have to utter in the same sentence: Property Taxes. BUYING: Two syllables homeowners can eradicate from their speech: land lord. (Notice how this latter term somehow becomes more archaic and sinister when separated into two words.) As a homeowner you can pretend that you are the master or mistress of your own domain.

• RENTING: You can expect your rent to increase incrementally a little bit every year. BUYING: Conversely, property values can increase or decrease wildly from minute to minute. Determining whether or not a property is a wise investment is exactly why you have a crystal ball. (And if you don't have one yet, purchase one immediately.)

• RENTING: When you rent, your neighbors can be particularly annoying. To deal with them, you can bang your broomstick against the ceiling or complain to the "lord of the land" (who will surely take your concerns into consideration). BUYING: As a homeowner, you can build a fence then romp maniacally behind it, occasionally flipping the bird in their direction. Just be prepared for them to sue you for installing the fence two millimeters into their property line.

• RENTING: One of the main benefits of renting is mobility – you can pretty much drop everything and go when a new whim or job opportunity beckons. BUYING: Then again, after a point, there's something to be said for knowing where you will live for the long haul and doing what you have to do to make it work (i.e. befriending a cadre of skilled roofers). It has been scientifically proven that there is only one thing worse than wading through all that mortgage gobbledygook and taking on all the responsibilities of ownership, and that, dear readers, is moving.

# How to Find Your Dream Home

Finding your dream home can be a long and arduous process. There are so many different styles of homes (i.e. Tudor, Colonial, Ranch, Condominium) and, depending on the previous owners, they can arrive on the market in many unfortunate states of disrepair (Dump, Shanty, Condemned Crack-Den, Haunted House Held Together only by Cobwebs). It's important to keep an open mind, while still honoring your dreams. It's also a good idea to carry a barf bag with you at all times, since not everyone has the same standards of cleanliness.

Here are a few other suggestions to assist in your search:

• Educate yourself by watching inordinate amounts of HGTV. You may not learn all the finer points of the transaction at HGTV University, but you will be alerted to a myriad of current trends. For example, a house is utterly worthless if it doesn't have both stainless steel appliances and granite countertops. (Note: we have neither.)

• Cast a wide net. Conscript the help of no less than 21 real estate agents in 16 states. How else are you going to figure out where you want to live? Just think of all the frequent flyer miles you will rack up.

• Be honest. Make sure the agents know you are undecided about location and have almost no money (Pre-approval? What's that?) The more pathetic you seem, the more motivated they'll be to help you.

• Compose a wish list at least seven miles long. And remember to be specific. For example, if you have a particular kitchen backsplash in mind, make sure to note the type, size, and color of the tiles. Then go out there and find a house with it!

• Judge a house by the current décor. After all, who wants to buy a home from people with bad taste? Conventional wisdom (a.k.a. HGTV) tells you to look past the current cosmetics. However, once you see a room with a stained shag carpet, jungle-frond wallpaper, and an extensive Precious Moments collection in the hutch, these images will be burned in your psyche, making it impossible to ever see this home as your own. Humans have seedy pasts they can't escape, and rooms do, too.

• If you start to get discouraged, spice up your search by wearing safari clothes. Pretend your car is a dune buggy and every new listing is an exotic creature that will both amaze and terrify you.

• Knock on every wall in an effort to identify studs and learn to ask the question, "Is this wall weight-bearing?" You never know, you may want to eventually open up the bathroom to the living room – open floor plans are all the rage right now.

• Inquire about ghosts. Realtors and sellers are obligated to disclose this key information. If there are in fact ghosts, this doesn't have to be a deal breaker. Just make sure you understand their personalities, policies, and proclivities. For example, if they are amiable ghosts with good dancing skills, the rest of your life could be a constant party.

• Some people claim you shouldn't let emotions play a role in your decision, but this is as ridiculous as saying you shouldn't let emotions influence your choice of a life partner. In other words, don't be frightened off by cracks in the foundation of a gorgeous house, mold in the basement, or an ancient furnace: if it's love, it's love. And good looks are all that really matter, anyway.

• Finally, if you have followed all of the above advice and still haven't found a place after taking tours of hundreds or even thousands of dumps/shanties/crack-dens, go ahead and buy the next one you see. Tear it down immediately and build exactly what you want. This isn't what we did, but according to HGTV, re-building and re-modeling a house is a snap. And even if the crew isn't composed of a bunch of ripped Aussies, and even if they take longer than they do on TV, camping out on your property for a few years will be fun!

# How to Spend Your Time While Waiting for the Closing

Once the contract is signed by both parties, it's supposedly a done-deal, but the (shag) rug could still get pulled out from under you. Paranoia is your best bet, here. Though our closing period was the slowest six months of my life, I managed to fill the time with all kinds of new obsessive-compulsive behaviors. If you are also feeling anxious, try some of these:

• Nervously bite your nails until they bleed. If there's a sudden, inexplicable, scarcity of pens across the universe (it could happen, especially with your luck), at least you'll still be able to sign your name on closing day.

• Call the sellers every seven minutes to make sure that they're still going to let you buy the place. Even though backing out would cost the sellers a great deal of money, it's a good idea to double and triple check.

• Invite the inspector out for drinks and ply him with extremely strong alcoholic beverages. Ask repeatedly, "So, really, is it a solid house?" You may also want to get a lie detector test involved. Most police stations are happy to loan out theirs for this purpose.

• Send weekly gift baskets to the mortgage broker.

• If your mortgage broker claims that "there's some hair on the deal" (true story – I guess banks don't trust freelancers), then offer to pay for financial electrolysis immediately.  If he can't shave away the complications, briefly consider getting a real job. (Scratch that last part – real jobs, especially in corporate America, are far too unstable these days, so that's really not the responsible thing to do at all.)

• When you are starting to feel hopeful (probably only a few days before the closing date), begin a serious workout regimen involving lots of heavy lifting. Even though you vowed, after that last move, to "hire it out," there will still be plenty of boxes and large pieces of furniture to lift (preferably with your back, while keeping your legs very straight – you don't want to blow out one of your knees).

• Take an acting class or hire a private acting coach to help you hit exactly the right emotional pitch for that moment when the keys are passed across the lawyer's table. When your agent finally says, "It's yours," no amount of drama is too much: tears should obviously be shed, appreciative kisses should be served all around, and you should perform a lengthy monologue about how this closing has, quote, opened the door to the rest of your life. Alternatively, you can just casually toss the keys in your bag, and embark on the long road to buyer's remorse without enjoying any fanfare.

# What to Do with Your 54,353 Page Mortgage Agreement

If you are able to decipher all that mortgage mumbo jumbo, then kudos – you are the only person in the universe who has ever been able to do so. You should definitely get a high-quality T-shirt printed up that advertises this fact.

On the other hand, if you are intimidated by that bulky pile of papers, just know that there are many other uses:

• Door Stopper

• Stepping Stool

• Sleep Aid: No more sleeping pills for you! Can you say bor-ing?

• Alarm clock: Rig your mortgage agreement to your nightstand so that it catapults into your lap if you ever try to reach for your telephone in order to call in "tired" to work. This will give you a scary jolt more powerful than 1000 coffees: if you lose your job, how on earth are you going to pay that hefty mortgage every month for the next 30 years?! PLUS taxes! You'll never be even a few minutes late to work ever again.

• Ego Deflation: If you ever experience one of those fleeting moments when you think you are actually intelligent, just open up to page one and try to understand three sentences. This will likely be as unsuccessful as the first 42 attempts. And voila! You're ego is right back to its diminutive size.

• Kindling

## Hosting a Housewarming Party

Even if you're not usually the type to host parties, you absolutely have to throw yourself a housewarming party. This is so you can receive useful gifts, like potholders and rare varieties of cacti. But there's another more important reason: so that your friends see why you took on that third job, and why they'll therefore never see you again. In a way, your housewarming will be a little like a farewell party, too.

Here's how to do it right:

• Make sure to add those last minute touches, like a welcome mat and a working toilet.

• Give exhaustive tours every hour on the hour, during which you explain everything you've done to the place, everything you plan to do, and all the deep psychological holes you are trying to fill in the process.

• If your fear of public speaking makes you uncomfortable with the concept of giving tours, suggest a game of Hide and Seek. This will give people the chance to see every nook and cranny of your place while in the process of both hiding and seeking.

• Put out an impressive spread composed mostly of finger foods. Try to keep the salmonella to a minimum, otherwise people might have a negative association with your home for the rest of their lives.

• Avoid serving beets, grape juice, and vats of blueberry compote. Because if somebody were to trip and fall into another person, who in turn fell into another person, and so on, the ensuing domino effect would result in dining room tie-dye. (Then again, you hadn't yet decided what motif you were going to go with in there...)

• Put out a bowl of Fortune cookies containing the following customized message: *If you donate to your friend's mortgage fund, you will be rewarded with infinite gratitude.* Though this could be interpreted as rather *gauche*, and probably won't put much of a dent in your mortgage, it might help defray the costs of this pricey shindig.

• Out of respect for your new neighbors, keep the volume on low. Don't hire your favorite speed metal band to perform or, for that matter, the Taiko drummers of Japan. If you put some classic rock on the radio very softly, everyone will be subliminally reminded of those innocent times when we all roamed free, without responsibilities.

• Ask all guests to remove their shoes upon entering. After all, you don't want your new carpet, tile, or freshly polished cement to get all scuffed up by their stilettos or sullied by their mangy sneakers. On second thought, their bare feet could actually do more damage from a filth perspective. Best to provide everyone with new socks, kind of like party favors (non-slip, of course – you don't want a lawsuit on your hands so soon out of the home-owning gate).

# 2. DESIGN

So you have your place – what are you going to fill it with? Maybe you have inherited lots of stylish furnishings, or you've been lugging around some lumpy pieces since college. Maybe you're going to use your new digs as a way to start fresh, decoratively speaking. Whichever way you go, rest assured that you don't have to spend a lot of money. That is, unless you want your home to look nice.

# What Your Design Choices
## Say about You

Even if you are a social person and love to entertain, you will realistically only have people over to your house less than eight times per year. Everyone's busy and it takes a lot to clean up, both before and after a gathering. But what your friends and family see when they visit will speak volumes about who you really are. So it's important that you choose your color scheme, décor, and furnishings with great care.

The following design choices will succinctly express your innermost self:

(Note: entries marked with an asterisk represent my own design predilections.)

• Red walls: "I have a heart. Blood courses through my veins. I love with abandon and sometimes experience intense rage."

• Oatmeal tones, such as beige, khaki, off-white and taupe: "Even though I am a big ball of nervous energy, I seek serenity and inner peace. I can get through my day only if I imagine myself relaxing on a beach on a clear afternoon. Now hurry up, we're late for spin class!"

• Safari Prints: "I have never left the country, but Marshalls and TJ Maxx have such great deals on exotic throw pillows."

• Minimalism: "My parents are hoarders so I do not believe in material objects, including furniture. Trust me, sitting on the floor to pay bills and leaning against the kitchen counter to eat dinner is better than body surfing on 36 years of magazine subscriptions just to get from the bedroom to the front door."

• Polka dots: "I had acne as a child, but I learned to love myself." *

• Dark wood and wallpaper in rich tones: "I will someday have enough money to retire. In the mean time, I will surround myself with the trappings of wealth. Do you have a couple thousand I can borrow for an interesting investment my cousin told me about from jail?"

• Overflowing bookshelves, a collection of owl figurines: "I am an intelligent person, despite my performance on standardized tests." *

• Asian Explosion: "Buddha is my BFF and I think this trifecta of Chinese characters means either *Laugh, Live, Eat* or *Dumplings Sold Here.* "

• Mid-Century Modern: "I wish I had lived in the 1950's, except for all that inequality." *

• Antique Chic: "Have I ever mentioned that I am related to a Russian prince, a woman named Marie Antionette, and also Cornelius Vanderbilt?"

• Cute-n-Country: "Howdy! I'd rather be dead than unfriendly."

## Guide to Garbage Pickin'

There is no shame in garbage picking. After all, one man's trash is another man's treasure. Some of my favorite pieces of furniture are items I plucked straight off the street on garbage day.

Though some might shudder at the thought of procuring things in this manner, others are proud to have made it a habit. Garbage picking is cost effective and only slightly disgusting. But there is a science to it.

Here are some recommendations:

• Keep your eyes open on garbage day: In other words, troll around in a large creepy van in the early hours of the morning while wearing a pair of rubber gloves and a lifting belt. Actually, most pickin's are spotted on the fly, when least expected, at a moment when staking claim and transport is most inconvenient. So, yeah, just keep your eyes open.

• Make sure the item is not in use: For example, if you stumble upon an awesome chair at 3 AM, make sure to look in all directions — north, south, east, west — to confirm that it is not currently in use. Even if it's tipped sideways beside garbage bins, it's possible that someone just stepped away, briefly. Your demeanor should clearly say, "Anyone sitting here?"

• Act with great stealth: Even if you are clearly the only person around for miles, be quick about it. You don't want to get involved in a tug-o-war with a garbage picker who has equally good taste.

• Stand sentry if necessary: If the item is too large to stuff into your pocket, your backpack, or to balance on your head, you will have to call in reinforcements and possibly a large vehicle. Waiting for assistance could take a while, so be prepared to guard your treasure Buckingham Palace style, minus the fluffy black Q-tip hat.

• Beware of Bed Bugs: Obviously soft products like couches, mattresses, and bed sheets should be avoided. These nasty intruders can ruin your whole day (or week, or year...)

• Wash, wash again, and wash at least one more time to be safe: in fact, wash all found objects 100 times to be safe. This isn't Obsessive Compulsive Disorder, it's common sense.

• Do not perform a sniff test before engaging in multiple washings: you will probably not like what you find. Along these lines, it is recommended that you discover your pickin's *before* the neighborhood dogs do, if you know what I mean.

• Respect your pickin's: In other words, if you have to put your belongings in storage during some sort of transitional period, don't discard your garbage pickin's just because it feels strange to pay good money to store free things. For example, I was separated from my pickin's for a long time – when we re-united, emotions ran so high that the Hallmark Channel asked if they could film a reenactment. I declined – nobody exploits my pickin's but me.

# How to Decorate a White Couch

For those of you who are undecided about your color scheme or intimidated by the interior design process, allow me to recommend a white couch. While some might argue that this object is too pristine and impossible to get comfortable on, it is actually one of the best purchases we have ever made. You'll find out pretty quickly that it is as versatile as a blank canvass, and fun, too.

With a white couch in the middle of your room, your palette can evolve organically over time. And you'll be amazed by your own artistic talents.

Here are some decorative suggestions, but feel free to explore your own techniques – the possibilities are infinite:

• Salsa: This plops very easily from the corner of a tortilla chip and smears beautifully with a paper towel.

• Red Wine: The way this sloshes over the lip of a wine glass is truly exquisite, especially if you watch the whole event as if it is happening in suspenseful slow motion. A dishtowel and a bit of water will transform this to a lovely mauve shade.

• Chicken Tikka Masala: Order this from your local Indian restaurant, bring it home then fill your favorite bowl with its fragrant goodness. Then allow a piece of delectable chicken to somehow explode almost geyser-style from your fork in a way that defies gravity and could never ever be repeated. The combination of yellow, orange and red exotic spices is indelible and becomes even more vibrant with the application of stain remover.

• Young Children: Invite several over to your house then provide them with lots of paint, crayons and magic markers. Laugh naively when their parents offer to write you a blank check for impending damages.

• Chocolate Chips: This one is a bit more complicated. Gobble chocolate chip cookies with a wild enthusiasm you learned from the Cookie Monster. This should result in several chocolate chips falling onto your lap. Get up, sit back down on top of them, and allow your body heat to melt them into the fibers of the couch for a rich, abstract mocha design.

• Moth: If it ever stops flitting around, press it into the cushion with the back of your hand in order to achieve an interesting charcoal-colored smudge. (Of course this is cruel, but wasn't it also cruel when he snacked his way through four of your favorite sweaters?)

• New Blue Jeans: Buy the darkest kind, the ones that leave dye on your fingers the first few times you wear them. Sit down and shift around a little bit. The result will be a gorgeous sky-blue splotch in the shape of your rear end.

• Extra Slip Covers: This one is key. Decide *against* purchasing these when you get the couch, for financial reasons, and only decide to buy them after both the couch and the slipcovers have both been discontinued. This is the only way you will develop enough commitment to (and pride in) all the work you have done, above.

# House Plant Psychology

According to the ancient Chinese art of *Feng Shui*, houseplants help to create a positive flow of energy throughout a house. On the other hand, dead or dying plants have the opposite effect. Of course, keeping them alive and healthy can feel like an uphill battle. Water, sun and the correct soil are obvious things to provide for your houseplants, but caring for them is actually far more complex than this. Though some might suggest a degree in Botany, what you really need is a Psychology degree, or maybe a Masters in Social Work, because it's all psychological.

Case in point: When I was growing up, my mother cut out and framed a cartoon from the newspaper with a woman standing next to her wilted plants. The caption reads: "Was it something I said?"

The answer is, yes, it was likely something she said, or maybe even something she didn't say.

Here are some tips on how to *not* become an owner of dead plants:

• Reverse Psychology: "Frankly, I don't care whether you prosper or not. It doesn't matter to me whether you are wilted or perky. In fact, drooping suits you."

• Healthy Competition: (To the fern) "Are you going let that measly little jade grow taller than you? And Aloe told me he's going try and grow two more inches by next week. They're all going to be bigger than you pretty soon – how is *that* going to feel?"

• Guilt trip: "I didn't get my thumbs tattooed green for nothing!"

• Threats: "I can go pick up a whole fleet of fake plants any time I want, and those don't require any of this high maintenance TLC."

• Motherly Nagging: "Please sit up, dear. Your posture looks terrible."

• Hypnosis: (Waving a pocket watch back and forth) "You're getting verrrry green."

• Tough Love: "Look, we come into this world alone, and we leave it alone. What you make of your time on this plant-stand is up to you."

• Guided Visualization: "Inhale. Imagine that you're in a rainforest, lush and verdant. Exhale. You are surrounded by friends. Inhale. A light mist covers your leaves. Exhale. If you work hard enough and do your share, you'll protect yourself and your family from deforestation. Inhale. Only *you* can save the forest. Exhale. But no pressure."

• Militancy: "Fifteen stretches! Now! And I don't want to hear all this bellyaching – if you think that's what plants did back in 'Nam, you got another thing coming!"

• Begging: (Get on your hands and knees and let a few real tears fall down your cheeks.) "Please?"

(Disclaimer: I have only ever been able to motivate one type of plant with the above methods and that is the extra hardy Philadendron. I have pushed many of them to the edge then talked them off the sill. My husband, on the other hand, has two real green thumbs, without tattoos.)

# How to Know When Your TV is too Large

There was a time when people spent their time at home reading books. There was a time when people ate dinner around a table, played charades, and made love. People used to even converse about the topics of the day. That was until televisions were invented. Ever since then, we've been hypnotized by the moving pictures to the exclusion of almost all other activities.

Of course, this development has had an impact on interior design. It used to be that the fireplace was a living room's primary focal point, or maybe a large picture window with a nice view. Chairs would be situated around these design features to maximize viewing pleasure. Now, everything faces the TV. Even the plants will grow in the TV's direction in order to get a better look.

Televisions have changed shape over the years – they were once fat and now they are thin, but they have also become taller and wider, as if afflicted by some kind of technological giantism. The result is that all of us are obsessed with getting bigger screens.

But take precaution, because there really can be too much of a good thing and your nicely shaped rooms are in danger of losing all sense of balance and proportion.

Here's how to know when your TV is too large:

• In order for it to fit, you have to build an addition onto your living room and/or lift your ceiling another 14 feet.

• The pores on your local newscaster's face are the size of dinner plates.

• The wall collapses when you try to hang the TV. When it crashes to the floor, it creates a minor earthquake felt around the block.

• You have to get rid of your refrigerator, your front door and your only full bathroom in order to make room for it.

• The nearby movie theater calls you in a panic when their electricity goes out to see if they can send their customers over to your house.

• Your remote control is actually a cockpit, larger and more complex than an airplane's.

# 3. GARDENING AND YARDENING

For those of you who have purchased condos, co-ops, or townhomes without yards, feel free to skip this chapter and enjoy your weekend, while the rest of us toil endlessly on our lawns and gardens so they don't become too bedraggled. Better yet: can you come over and lend a hand? These gardening gloves are one-size-fits-all.

For those of you who have outside property to attend to, some condolences are in order. Your lower back will never be the same from all that weeding, nor will your opinion of nature. (What once seemed so pretty and idyllic very suddenly becomes quite the opposite.) You *could* trim all your trees down to nubs and pour cement over your lawn, but then your home will begin to look a little too much like the prison that it is. Okay, that's a little melodramatic: maybe just embrace yard work, a.k.a. yardening, as your new form of exercise (and get a masseuse on speed dial).

Note: There are not very many tips on gardening per say, in this chapter, since I do not yet know much about this subject. The focus, therefore, is more on yard work, on which I am an "expert."

Another note: The word expert is in quotes.

# How to Motivate Yourself to Mow the Lawn

Bravo! That rain dance you did was not only highly entertaining to everyone in the neighborhood, but it had an effect — your lawn is now extremely green. Unfortunately, it is also now growing at an alarming rate. As soon as you finish cutting it, it starts growing again behind your back. You can try to ignore it, but the longer it gets, the more difficult it is to mow.

Here's how you can get yourself motivated:

• Convince yourself that your white sneakers would look so much better green: grass makes a nice natural dye.

• Pretend your lawn is a carpet and you get to design the pattern: Diagonal stripes? Rectangles? Concentric crop circles?

• Actually sit down and read that pile of hate mail the neighbors have been leaving in your mailbox. Maybe your laziness *is* bringing the neighborhood down. Then again, shouldn't they actually be thanking you for making them look good, relatively speaking?

• Note that lawn mowers are also excellent shredders. For example, if you live on a relatively busy street, there's probably no end to the litter discarded on your lawn, and constantly picking up after others quickly becomes a drag. Fortunately, your mower will make short work of paper bags and candy wrappers. Of course, beware: soda cans, beer bottles, and discarded mattresses will make short work of the mower.

• Imagine that you're a barber and your lawn is the client. He came in heavy metal and wants to leave with a buzz cut. (Keep in mind: he's not a great tipper.)

• Remember that it's nice to be able to see out the windows: if you let the grass grow much longer, you'll lose your view of the neighbor's pool. (Oh wait, that could be a relief, for several reasons.)

# How to Get Poison Ivy

Getting Poison Ivy is extremely easy! Just follow these steps:

• To get a poison ivy (or poison oak, or poison sumac) rash, the first thing you need to do is not live in a city. Move to the country, or the suburbs, at least, where there is a nice green-to-cement ratio.

• When you notice that the previous owners of your new house left behind a spray bottle of Poison Ivy Killer in your basement, pause momentarily and say to yourself: "That must mean there is poison ivy around these parts." Then, don't give it another thought.

• Undertake a clean-up project in the part of your garden that has become far more wild and jungle-like since you moved in.

• Make sure you tackle this project in your skimpiest bikini, or speedo, or if you are feeling really motivated: naked. Whatever you do, *do not* wear gloves, shoes, or socks. (Note: this is also an excellent way to attract deer ticks.)

• Remain unclear about exactly what poison ivy looks like. Remember vaguely that it has three leaves, but almost every plant you are pulling out of the ground (then rolling around in) fits that description.

• Schedule your clean-up project on the hottest day of the year. This way, when you wipe the sweat off your brow, you can transfer the poison ivy oil from your hands to your face. While you're at it, run your hands thoroughly all over your body as if you are applying some kind of soothing lotion. (You will need lots of practice at this in order to get through the next few weeks.)

• Along these same lines, take a shower immediately, so that water can carry the poisonous oil to any part of your body that you missed previously.

• Be patient: poison ivy doesn't show up immediately. Trust that the painful, itchy blisters will appear soon enough.

• Time your outbreak so that it has the most impact: schedule it so that the rash is at its most raging during your wedding, an important business conference, or your high school reunion.

• When your poison ivy rash clears up completely, repeat above.

Now get out there!

# What to Do if You Find an Egg in Your Yard

What should you do if you find a perfect little egg in your yard the day after Easter?

• Marvel at the wonders of the natural world.

• Decide it looks a little *too* perfect to be real and assume it had to have been manufactured in a factory. Perhaps it blew off an Easter decoration or fell out of the basket of a very busy bunny.

• Eagerly pick it up to see if it has jellybeans inside, and discover in the process that it seems more real than synthetic.

• Instantly regret contaminating it with your human hands and remember that this means the mother will mostly likely reject it (if she hasn't done so already).

• Wonder how you can de-contaminate it. (Anti-bacterial gel? Bleach? Soft Scrub works well on a lot of things.) Realize that turning back time would probably be more feasible.

• Look around for the nest it may have originated from. If you can't find it, gather together some sticks, yarn, and various yard bits in order to construct a stylish nest, or maybe a nifty crib that will eventually transition to a toddler bed.

• Vow to raise this bird as if she's your very own and give her the best opportunities life has to offer while of course teaching her where she came from.

# The Finer Points of Leaf Removal

If you live anywhere that enjoys the four seasons, the changing of the leaves in the fall will turn your property into a magical colorfest. Soon thereafter, though, you will have a big mess. Isn't it a bit disrespectful the way the trees just let their leaves *fall* to the ground for others to pick up?

Though it seems like a great idea to install "NO LEAVES" signs all over your lawn (i.e., a leaf with a red slash through it), I can tell you from experience that this unfortunately doesn't work. Those irreverent trees probably don't follow crosswalk rules either.

The sooner you understand the finer points of leaf removal the better. They are as follows:

• Even though you swore you never would, go ahead and invest in the most evil of suburban contraptions: a leaf blower. After all, why rake when you can let air do the work? Why just get blisters on your hands when you can also permanently damage your eardrums?

• Leaf blowers are LOUD: make sure to wear that sexy ear protection that looks like a cross between earphones and earmuffs.

• Accept that leaf blowing does not magically solve your leaf situation. Surprisingly, even if you have a leaf blower, it is still necessary to go old-school and employ the use of a rake for escorting/cajoling/coaxing leaves in the desired direction

• FYI: It takes approximately four minutes and 33 seconds of raking for blisters to appear on your palms even while wearing sensible yardening gloves.

• Dry leaves in an organized pile + heavy wind = leaf party. And all of your hard work is, poof, suddenly undone. Your lawn once again looks to be strewn with trash and confetti, much like 34th Street after the Macy's Thanksgiving Day Parade.

• Finally, the energy output and navigational math required for all of the above is compounded when your neighbors are blowing their leaves onto your property. The etiquette here is admittedly murky: maybe *their* leaves are actually *your* leaves since they came from your trees? Still, it is a strange and slightly offensive sight to see them blowing them in your direction.

# How to Justify Lawn Ornamentation

Let's face it, pretty much *all* lawn ornamentation is kitschy and tacky, no matter how you look at it. And yet, as soon as you own a home with a yard, you will probably feel a strange desire to incorporate some into your landscape. This might, rightfully so, lead to some feelings of shame and embarrassment.

The absolute best way to justify all forms of lawn ornamentation is through irony, i.e. "I am just being ironic." If this fails to make you feel better about yourself, here are some more specific justifications:

• Pink Flamingo: If you live in a warm clime, such as Florida, you are just doing what you can to fit in, and assimilation is a healthy human inclination. On the other hand, if you don't live in a warm climate, you are displaying a very understandable wish fulfillment. These are the most ironic of all lawn ornaments, but there is a practical aspect: if you have no gardening skills and can't seem to produce any roses, daisies, or peonies of any shade, a plastic pink flamingo brings a nice pop of color to your otherwise bland space.

• Reflective Gazing Globes: Whether or not you are actually a wizard, this will give passersby the definite impression that you are. And haven't you been yearning to seem a little more mysterious? You can further create intrigue by starting to wear a velvet cloak with stars embroidered on it. An added benefit is that these balls are so reflective, you can use yours as one final "do I have food in my teeth?" checkpoint as you leave for work.

• Dragonfly on a stick: Depending what sources you consult, dragonflies represent just about everything under the sun…courage, happiness, strength, swiftness, luck, rebirth, and the list goes on. If you have an XL dragonfly on a stick at the front of your house, it can serve the same purpose as a political endorsement sign. As in: "I am pro Luck." Or "We, at this household, endorse Happiness." Or "Vote Courage."

• Country Duck: All country ducks make a nice statement about your reverence for simpler times, when small farms dotted the countryside and ducks waddled free. But the best types of country duck lawn ornaments are the ones that come with a wardrobe: i.e. yellow slicker, Santa suit, sundress, leprechaun vest, etc., depending on the season. This might prevent you from dressing up your dog in similar garb. It might also help your children to dodge a few bullets in the wayward costume department. (Note: no guarantees on either of these last claims.)

• Lawn Jockies Holding a Lantern: Nope, sorry, no justification for this one.

• Garden Gnomes: Gnomes are the best kind of lawn ornamentation. They are responsible, very hardworking (just look at those heavy boots) and perfectly tidy, with their belts in place and their hats coming to a perfect point. Sure, most gnomes drink too much and they spend inordinate amounts of time grooming their beards in the wizard ball, but they always manage to be punctual. Incidentally, if you no longer have a grandfather or he lives far away, gnomes bring a nice grandfatherly vibe to the place by exuding a sense of authority and gravitas.

• Cherub Statues: A cherub, like a gnome, will help you pretend that you are being watched over and protected, to some degree. More importantly, her scantily-clad rolls of fat will remind you to go to the gym on a daily basis. Beware, however: cherubs are usually flirts and know no boundaries. If she runs off with the flamingo, the dragonfly, or the country duck, don't say you weren't warned.

# 4. THE ART OF THE MEMO

No matter where you live, critters seem to gather 'round, some friendly, others less so. It's hard to corner them for a conversation – they're busy, you're busy and the chances of mis-communicating in an actual conversation are far too high. This is why it's important to develop the art of writing memos to resident spiders, freeloading geckos, and interloping insects of all kinds. These get your point across clearly and decrease the chances for misunderstandings.

Besides, whenever a potential disagreement is brewing, they say you should leave a so-called paper trail. You don't have to be a lawyer to know that a well-written memo is adequate evidence in a court of law. Be sure to make copies for your files. And if you really want to be thorough homeowner, get a notary involved.

Some examples follow. Feel free to use these verbatim or as templates for your own specific purposes.

# Memo to the Ants in the Mailbox

To: Ants
From: Us

This is just to let you know that tampering with other people's mail is a federal offense.

It is a crime to walk, jig, or hold raves on mail intended for anyone but yourself.

It is furthermore uncool for you to sneak into other people's envelopes and read the contents aloud while snickering then act all nonchalant and suspiciously busy with "other things" when the addressees open the mailbox door.

Likewise, ordering items from catalogues addressed to others as if you are them is a form of identity theft and is not appreciated no matter how nice those products turn out to be. (That set of watermelon flavored patio furniture is certainly unique, but, come on – those shipping fees?)

If riding a piece of mail as if it's a magic carpet is your way of infiltrating our home so that you can walk in confident diagonal paths across our kitchen counter, just know that we applaud your ingenuity. But we don't like it.

Finally, our mailbox is private property and we do not welcome squatters. We do, however, understand the urge to hold meetings and/or parties in clubhouse settings i.e. tree houses (and in your case, elevated mail receptacles) so we are willing to negotiate a rental agreement.

Please get back to us via mail at your earliest convenience.

# Memo to the Fruit Flies

To: The Fruit Flies
From: Us

Look, we're bigger than you, stronger than you, faster than you. And we know where you live. Wait, that's not true: where *do* you live?

We are not really familiar with your customs or habits. As far as we knew, you focused most of your loitering efforts on bunches of old bananas.

But since we spotted the first of you, we have gotten rid of all the fruit in the house. We moved our trash to a secret location three miles away. We wrapped our strawberry jam in cellophane and snapped it inside a plastic container before locking it in a safety deposit box. Even the night guard we hired to stand by the refrigerator door is stumped. Because, still, you're here, and not concentrated in any one place, but seem to making yourself comfortable all over our house.

For the record, I don't appreciate when you hover in front of my face while I'm trying to watch television, when you balance along the rim of my coffee cup, or try to upstage me in front of my own make-up mirror.

By the way, we think you have a drinking problem: you should be ashamed of the way you flocked to my glass of wine the other night. That bottle was not cheap. (Though you should be commended on the sophistication of your palettes.)

What we can never forgive you for is the way you embarrassed us during our dinner party last week. It was downright presumptuous of you to assume that you were invited. To see our guests swatting you off their garlic bread was horrifying and made us feel like the most disgusting humans on earth.

Maybe this is just your season to shine. I went out for breakfast the other day and there you were, buzzing around my head. I need to know: were you already at the restaurant, or did you follow me from home? I felt like Pig Pen from the Peanuts cartoon, except instead of dust, I had a cloud of fruit flies surrounding me.

Please go back to where you came from. Or, at the very least, tell us how you could be of use around here. For example, what talents can you bring to the table? If you can't contribute something useful, we have every right to request rent, with interest applied retro-actively.

Your response (or disappearance) is requested immediately.

## Memo to the Bunny

To: The Bunny
From: Us

We know that you have taken up residence in our front garden and we are thrilled that you are comfortable here.

We have just a few questions:

When we are at home, can you please hang out in plain sight more often and not hop back into the bushes so quickly when we walk out the front door? This hurts our feelings: we would like to observe you/hang out with you/at least snap a picture of you. In other words, can you chillax? Let's get to know each other!

When you are eating dinner, for example, speed-nibbling on grass – or consuming a whole dandelion, stem and all, at that impressive, rapid-fire pace – are you saying to yourself, "num-num-num-num-num-num"? This is what we think you are saying but we don't want to make any incorrect assumptions.

When we see you traveling from one bush to another, are you pretending that you live on a grand estate and that you are taking inventory of The Grounds? Because this is what we pretend when we hop around our property.

We've never seen you with anyone else and we were wondering if you are lonely? This past Easter, we adopted a pretty little bunny composed of glass — she's very cool, albeit somewhat fragile. You could probably learn a lot from her calm energy and open, almost transparent, manner. Let us know if you if you'd like us to introduce you.

Finally, can you stay your exact same size? Not that we want you to be stunted or underdeveloped, or that we will love you any less as a full-grown rabbit, but you're just so cute this small and this fluffy. And that fuzzy white tail of yours brings us more delight than we could possibly express in words.

Most importantly, please don't ever leave? If there is anything we can do to make your stay more enjoyable, just ask. You know where to find us.

# Memo to the Bumble Bees

To: The Bumble Bees
From: Us

We know that you have taken up residence in a hole right where the walkway meets our front garden. We have seen you entering and exiting and also hovering there. This is not an eviction notice and we are cool with you staying on the premises, but we have a number of questions we'd like to ask.

First, how many of you are there? We hate to insult your individuality, but we can't tell you apart, and according to our best estimates there are at least three of you and possibly as many as 100.

Along those same lines, are you familiar with the clown car gag? If not, this is a skit involving several clowns and one teeny car, usually performed on a television program more whacky than serious in nature. The joke is that there is no logical way so many clowns could possibly fit inside such a small vehicle. As a parade of too many clowns either enter or exit the car, it's hard to tell if this is a trick of the camera or if clowns are magically able to condense themselves when confronted with tight quarters. This is all to say that we have peered inside this little nest you have created with a flashlight, and we are similarly perplexed.

How exactly did you dig this hole? Was it with your bare hands/paws/wings/pads? (And what exactly is it that you have at the end of your arms/legs?) It seems, frankly, to be quite an impressive undertaking for creatures such as yourselves, without renting a backhoe or at least some shovels. Kudos!

We did some research with the help of a tool named Google. This led us to believe that you are a rather harmless species and will likely not attack us, sting us, or cause us to swell up like Martin Short did in the hilarious bee sting scene in the otherwise mediocre movie, *Pure Luck*.

Anyway, we hope you are the peace-loving creatures we presume you to be. If you prove to be a danger to us, then we may have to re-visit the concept of eviction.

In fact, the above-referenced research has caused us to refer to you as the "chubbier, friendlier bees." Does this offend you? We think you are cute, and we would hate for you to develop a complex about your appearance, but we have noticed that you are all rather thick around the middle. (For your information, studies have shown that extra weight around the waistline can increase the chance of heart disease. We've noticed also that you are rather slow-moving, which can be an indication of a low energy level possibly related to high cholesterol or increased blood pressure. We are not even sure of your diet and far be it for us to judge you, but you may want to cut back on whatever it is that you eat.)

Just curious: why horizontal stripes? Love the black and yellow color combination, but you may want to consider vertical lines, as they are commonly thought to create a more slimming appearance.

Do you speak the same dialect as wasps by any chance? If so, can you tell them they are not welcome in our house? We have attempted to get this message across, but something is obviously getting lost in the translation.

Did you know that human children, especially babies and toddlers, love to dress up as you during Halloween? Do you guys ever dress up as humans or as anything else on that day? If you ever need any costume ideas, we can help out – that's one of our favorite holidays! Oh, here's a good one: how about wearing grey sweatsuits with the words Good Year printed along your side? You know, like the Good Year blimp? There is a great costume parade in town – we should all go!

# Memo to the Crickets

To: Crickets
From: Us

Help! We are so confused. We understand that the media regularly misrepresents situations and takes all kinds of gross liberties with the truth. But we just can't comprehend why the sound of chirping crickets is so often used to represent a silence more profound than silence itself.

For example, say a character on a sitcom is at a loss for words and can't seem to explain why he just accidentally answered the door wearing only a frilly apron? Cue the sound of chirping crickets. Bloated woman asks her girlfriends if her pants look too tight? Chirping crickets.

Likewise, chirping crickets are often used to set the scene in a nature narrative: a couple from the city finally gets away for a night of camping. Ahh... the sweet song of the forest.

Here's the thing: that sound you make? It's actually very loud and incredibly annoying, no matter what any advertisement, movie or TV show might suggest. And it only takes about a minute and a half to for it to bore XL holes in a pair of high-end earplugs.

Look, for all we know, you are guys are seasoned professionals, highly respected for your craft. Maybe you're rehearsing for the largest production of *La Boheme* ever staged in the long and venerable history of insect operas. Maybe it's some kind of religious chant. Far be it from us to censor you.

But can you take it down a notch or at least move it elsewhere? We can't figure out exactly where you are located – By the front door? In the attic? Inside our heads? Wherever you are, can you go further away? Why don't you commandeer that wooded area behind our house, far from our bedroom window, for your rehearsal space?

And while we're on a roll with suggestions: you might also want to consider changing up that tune slightly – 152 straight hours of that two-note melody doesn't exactly speak to your creativity.

Really, all we ask is that you see things from our perspective for a moment: we moved to this freestanding house in the suburbs in order to escape the random screams, honking taxis, and a panoply of loud upstairs neighbors (i.e. elephants, aspiring tap dancers, and professional door slammers). We were looking for a little peace and a lot of quiet.

The first night, after we got everything moved into this, our new home, we sat down with a glass of wine and a celebratory cigar, respectively. We looked at each other with relief. And then we heard a sound that wasn't anything like silence, not even close.

Please take pity on us, for we are fragile. Our hearing is, as of now, excellent. And we have a long way to go on this mortgage.

# 5. COPING WITH EMERGENCIES

Surely your house was constructed with quality materials and solid engineering. Unfortunately, however, even the sturdiest structures (and individuals) are vulnerable to disasters, such as earthquakes, floods, brushfires and roach infestations, to name just a few. It's important to always be prepared for *all* conceivable catastrophes, even though the possibilities are infinite. Don't worry, we've researched the best ways to be proactive and reactive – we are more than happy to share them with you in the following pages.

Note: The disasters addressed herein are only the tip of the iceberg. Speaking of which, beware of icebergs.

# How to Prepare for a Hurricane

If a hurricane is coming your way, the best thing you can do is get in your car and leave the area ASAP. Be sure to first retrieve your most cherished items from your home, like your antique button collection and your funniest refrigerator magnets. Don't forget the manuscript of the loosely autobiographical novel you'll probably never finish writing anyway (though a hurricane could provide that exciting plot twist you've been waiting for…)

The thing is, despite the sophistication of modern meteorological technology, it's difficult to tell *exactly* how bad the storm is going to be and if it's actually going to hit your beloved abode. Besides, how can you protect your home (or even know what's happening to it) from a hotel room two hours away? So, unless you are officially forced to evacuate, it's understandable if you make the stupid decision to stay.

Here is what you should do in preparation:

• Develop new hand-wringing techniques: That one you usually use is going to get very boring very fast in this situation, so try out a circular motion in the opposite direction, a little side to side action, and maybe get the fingers involved in a more innovative way. Better yet, choreograph all of these together into an entertaining routine.

• In order to batten down the hatches, first find out what a hatch is, then take a class on how to batten.

• Do a shot of something alcoholic every time a local newscaster uses the phrase "hunker down." After all, if your house is going to get sloshed, you might as well, too.

• If your panic attacks are less than five minutes apart and last for more than 60 seconds, head immediately to the emergency room because you are about to give birth to a big ball of anxiety. Congratulations are in order – hopefully the nursery you stenciled with skulls and crossbones won't get ruined in the storm.

• Pull all of your patio furniture and lawn ornamentation inside – otherwise, they will become projectiles and this could be very awkward. For example, if your garden gnome flies through your neighbor's bathroom window at an inopportune time, the damage to his sanity (the gnome's) (ok, and the neighbor's…) could be irreparable.

• Secure the trees around your house by leaning your body weight up against them: keep changing your position depending on which way the wind is blowing. Don't be discouraged by the fact that you can only save one tree at a time in this way. It is important to stay focused during catastrophes. (Note: if this does not work, consult "If a Tree Falls on Your House," next.)

• Stock up on batteries and flashlights, because your electricity is bound to go out and anything scary is 100 times *more* scary in the dark. (Do not light candles under any circumstances. For more information, see "Keeping an Eye on Resale" at the end of this guide.) You may want to hire the services of professional fireflies as back-up. It is a little known fact that some fireflies light up for fun and others work on an hourly basis. (Fees vary, depending on where you are located in the country.)

• Fill your gas tank: This is less for escape than for charging your cell phone and listening to the radio. They say that good music does wonders for the psyche.

• In preparation for flooding, take everything out of your basement and line the floor with layers of ultra-absorbent diapers. Of course, reserve a few for personal use, just in case your plumbing also buckles under the pressure.

• In the nights leading up to the storm, sit up in bed, tense and worrying (this is a good time to practice your newest hand-wringing routine, as detailed, above) so that when the storm hits, you are completely exhausted. Take my word for it, this is the only way you'll have any hope of sleeping through it.

• Duck and cover: you might as well put to use something you learned in grade school.

# If a Tree Falls on Your House

Having a variety of trees on your property is a wonderful thing: they provide shade, atmosphere, and a nice habitat for birds. The older the trees are, the more charming. Unfortunately, aging trees, like aging humans, become increasingly frail. They are susceptible to disease and balance issues. As a result, trees sometimes fall down in high winds and extremely wet conditions. The only thing you can really hope for is that if a tree does fall, it falls away from your house, away from the neighbor's house, away from the street, away from your car, and away from any pedestrians who happen to be walking by. Sadly, there is only a .000000003 percent chance that it will miss all of these targets.

You know that age-old question – if a tree falls in the woods and no one is there to hear it, does it make a sound? People can debate each side of this all day long. But we learned during one storm that when a tree falls on your house, the answer is extremely clear: yes, it makes a very loud sound, practically deafening. Furthermore, it will be accompanied by the sound of millions of coins suddenly spilling out of your bank account.

Here is a handy checklist to use, if this situation *befalls* you:

• First, stay calm.

• Second, check to make sure that you are not pinned under the tree.

• Third, retroactively call out the warning "Timber!" as if this were the work of invisible lumberjacks and you're just trying to help out.

• Next, in order to keep the outside from seeping in, cover the hole the tree created with a tarp, or an XXXXXL shower cap, or that old tent you bought for camping 12 years ago but never used. Putting this in place might require a terrifying trip up to the roof. In this case, do not even think about standing, up there. Instead, just crawl around wearing baseball cleats on your hands and your knees in order to decrease slippage.

• Wonder if you ever got around to renewing your Homeowner's Insurance (or signing up for it in the first place).

• Curl up into a little ball and whimper for a good spell.

• Once your tear ducts are nice and dry, call the roofer and a licensed therapist.

• Finally, cut down all the trees on your property so that this can never ever happen again.

## How to Know When it's Time to Buy a Snow Blower

Mother Nature is a powerful and creative woman. She is also extremely moody and has a wicked sense of humor. She expresses these latter personality traits in different ways, depending on the season and depending on where you live in the country. In the winter months, in the northeast quadrant of the country, she dumps piles upon piles of heavy white stuff all over the place. It covers your driveway and quickly makes it impassable. The nice thing is that this gives you a perfectly acceptable excuse to not go to work. The tragedy is that pizza delivery personnel cannot access your house.

As a homeowner, the responsibility to remove this white stuff from your driveway and sidewalk is yours and yours alone. You can hope for it to melt (and eventually it will) but, before that, you're probably going to have suit up in your warmest clothes, your ugliest hat, and your waterproof boots in order to move it out of your way, one shovel-full at a time. That is, unless you have the good sense to invest in a snow blower. If you think that you're too hands-on, too un-suburban and just generally too cool to push that contraption around, you'll just have to learn your lesson the hard way.

Here's when you'll know for sure that its time:

• Your extensive shovel collection is ruined – all of them have either snapped like matchsticks or bent like cheap spoons.

• You have strained your shoulders to such a degree that lifting only one more snowflake will actually dislocate them.

• The only way to get out to your street is by catapulting yourself from a second floor window.

• Hollywood producers knock on your door and ask if they can film a sequel to *The Shining* at your house since it looks even more snow-logged and isolated than the hotel in the original movie.

• You haven't been out to the store in a long time and your rations are depleting: you're down to four peanuts and a tablespoon of mustard.

• You become delirious and hallucinatory: you look out at your snow-covered driveway and see a green field dotted with sunflowers. A cardinal waves at you and you only snap out of it when you notice that he's wearing earmuffs.

• Your neighbors have to cross-country ski across your yard to see if you are still alive.

# Before Tackling any DIY Projects

It's admirable to roll up your sleeves and tackle projects around the house with which you have absolutely no experience and for which you have even less aptitude. In theory, "doing it yourself" is cost-effective and enriching. In practice, it is often a disaster and extremely dangerous. Remember that many of the roads leading to homeowner's hell are paved with good intentions.

If, despite your better judgment, you are determined to take a DIY approach, even though you'd be wise to hire it out, at least do the following:

• Count your fingers, so you know exactly how many you had before starting the project.

• Put 911 on speed dial.

• Pray.

• Wear a hard hat even if you don't think its necessary: you never know what could happen when sewing curtains, sanding a chair, or repotting a plant.

• DIY a holster for your fire extinguisher so that it can be attached to your belt at all times.

• Hire a large corporate consulting firm to conduct a thorough cost and risk analysis. (In case you're unsure where to find this type of organization, one of the more reputable companies in this business is, *I Told You So, Inc.*)

• Take a photograph of the project in the "before" stage so that you can show this to the professional contractor when he or she comes to fix the mess you made.

# Your Security System:
# Peace of Mind and Worst Nightmare

Nice as it is to move from an apartment to a freestanding home, it can also be a little unsettling. There are so many points of entry: front doors, back doors, side doors, and low-slung windows so close to the ground that burglars can easily hop into them when you least expect. It can therefore be comforting to rig up an alarm system that will alert you to intruders. Hopefully, it will also scare them off, and automatically contact the police for you.

Here's the thing though: your alarm will also undoubtedly scare *you* to death. That sound it makes is deafeningly-loud. It will certainly induce panic, and there is a 79% chance that it will give you a heart attack.

The question you have to ask yourself is: what will you do when that alarm starts to go off? Here are some suggestions:

• Reach for your flashlight, baseball bat, mace, and stun gun. Spontaneously sprout two more arms so that you can hold (and possibly use) all of these items simultaneously.

• Call out: Who's there? Whether or not you are a man or a woman, lower your voice by 15 octaves in order to sound more threatening. Corollary benefit: this could be intriguing to the intruders if they just happen to be one baritone short of a barbershop quartet.

• Call out: Who trespass-eth herein? Dazzle the burglars with your medieval diction and syntax. Then offer them a stein of ale, a bowl of gruel and a whole leg of lamb – they'll be so confused by your hospitality and the time warp that they'll forget all about your huge flat screen. They'll also overlook your laptop collection and ignore your drawer filled with rare diamonds.

• Jump out the nearest window and run for your life. Don't worry if you are scantily clad, or wearing Hello Kitty pajamas – your safety is more important than your dignity. And your neighbors will be more likely to provide sanctuary if you provide them with a good laugh.

• Roll over and go back to sleep, assuming that, yet again, a mouse, spider, or bobcat has strolled across the living room sensor.

• Telephone the security company and apologize for accidentally tripping the system for the 27th time this week.

# Things that Do Not Discourage Mice

Of all possible catastrophes outlined in these pages, taking on mice as uninvited guests is the worst one of all. Basically, if mice make their way into your beloved house, there is only one thing to say: good luck. There's also only one consolation: at least they're not rats. And there's really only one way to deal with this pesky problem: accept it. Because there is absolutely nothing else you can do.

Here are some tactics you would like to think would get rid of them, but won't:

• Mouse traps set with cheese: This doesn't even work in cartoons.

• Mouse traps set with peanut butter: This is only alluring to them if they also get their paws on some bread and jelly. But even then, they are perfectly capable of a clean heist.

• Mouse traps with little roofs over the top: Don't insult them – they already have a roof over their heads…yours.

• Mouse traps made with extra sticky glue: This is the epitome of cruel – if you put one of these out, they will not only lose respect for you, they will seek revenge by doing unspeakable things to that open butter dish you always forget to put in the refrigerator.

• Strongly-worded memos: They can read, (and in fact have a grand ol' time acting out scenes from your diary while you're at work) but they ignore official documents. And, hence, this is why they were not addressed in the memo section of this guide. Likewise, don't even bother trying to give them bills for all the trouble they've caused you – they will simply shred them in order to make stuffing for tiny mattresses.

• Peppermint Oil: Go ahead and sprinkle it all over the floor, wash your hair with it and make lots of tea – they're just going to think you're crazy for believing this old wive's tale. If you're really hell-bent on peppermint, you're better off stabbing them with sharpened candy canes.

• Lazy, well-fed cats: Why chase when you can nap?

• Humans: Anybody to who says, "they're more afraid of you than you are of them" is unfortunately just plain wrong.

• Poison: They have stomachs of steel. That which does not kill them makes them stronger.

• Furniture: You may think you're safe up there on that table (and it *is* impressive how you can travel all the way from the kitchen counter to the couch to the bed without ever touching ground), but they're still far more agile than you and have no problem coming right up to where you are to join in the fun.

• Steel Wool: Sure, you can stuff it into every last crevice of your attic, floorboards, and basement, but chewing through it is one of their favorite past times. (Second only to the obstacle course created by the tussled sheets on your unmade bed.)

• Relocation: You can try to move away, but they enjoy burrowing into your box of underwear and making the trip. In fact, they're just as excited as you are to start anew.

# 6. GENERAL UP-KEEP

When you first moved into your new home, there was a wonderful honeymoon period. Everything seemed so sexy and sleek. You felt, for a while, as if you were "playing house," or as if you were being featured in a trendy home magazine.

But, as with any new situation, the sheen soon wears off, and you're eventually left with the sad fact that your dream house isn't always such a dream. You often feel as if you are under attack by the elements and various critters. Appliances that worked when you first moved in begin to betray you. And most horrifyingly, you realize that you can't escape yourself. In other words, you're a slob no matter where you go.

Keep in mind that, when you own a house, the stakes are high, since you may want to sell the place one day. So when you break something or ignore it to the point of ruin (say, for example, those mold growths on your bathroom tile too resilient for a jackhammer) you not only compromise your space, you compromise your entire future.

Don't worry, though, you will learn your lessons the way all homeowners in the history of houses have: by screwing up. Hopefully the advice in the following pages will make this imperfect process a little less painful.

# Daily Affirmations for Daily Chores

You may or may not know that chore-phobia (the fear of chores) is a real and very serious condition. Symptoms include laziness, procrastination, and various allergic reactions. Those who suffer from this ailment often feel sluggish and experience bouts of self-loathing. The good news is that there is a cure: it involves giving yourself pep talks on a daily (and even hourly) basis.

Before attempting any of the following affirmations, it's important to first acknowledge your situation and accept the duties that go along with it. Once you have done so, you can consider yourself a responsible homeowner, *and* a full-fledged and functioning adult human.

Note: All of the following affirmations are null and void if you have the means to hire help or if you cohabitate with someone who is willing to actually do all those annoying household chores. If either of these are the case, you are a very lucky individual. Don't lift a finger: your only obligation is to revel in your chore-phobia and milk it for all its worth.

• Dishes: "I am a civilized, evolved person. Eating from take-out containers with my hands because there are no clean dishes or utensils is beneath me. Besides, if I don't do the dishes, no one else will."

• Laundry: "I believe what my mother taught me – that cleanliness is next to Godliness. And, incidentally, God has not offered to wash my clothes. (Really, that's probably a good thing, because she tends to go a little heavy on the bleach.) In other words, if I don't do the laundry, no one else will."

• Trash: "I am strong enough to accomplish anything I set my mind to, including lugging 40 gallon bags of garbage the entire length of the driveway. Besides, wearing a nose plug all day is uncomfortable, spraying this much air freshener is costly, and constant varmint control is getting tiresome. I might as well go ahead and take out the trash, because no one else will."

• Recycling: "I am a magnanimous and environmentally conscious person. I am willing and able to sort through plastics, glass, and newspapers in order to re-purpose these materials, thereby protecting planet earth for future generations of excessive consumers. Besides, if I don't drag these bins out to street, no one else will."

• Sorting the Mail: "I deserve good fortune. While this pile, now four miles high, probably consists mostly of junk mail from shameless advertisers, there is also an infinitesimally small chance that, within that stack, there is a sweepstakes check for eight million dollars. And if I don't cash it, maybe someone else will."

# In Defense of Dirt and Dust

Sometimes even the most powerful affirmations can't help. For example, it doesn't matter what you say to yourself or how many times you say it, you're probably never going to want to deal with all the dirt and dust that builds up in your living space. The worst part is that it never ends: there's always a new mess to contend with and it's always coming at you from every direction. Even if you live like a hermit with the doors and windows always closed and without ever going anywhere, dust will find its way in. It's wily and unrelenting: it accumulates on, under, around, and even inside your possessions, both big and small.

Sure, the best plan of action is to clean it up. And it would be nice if you could motivate to do so, but cleaning any house larger than two rooms is a daunting task. Keeping the entire place dust- and dirt-free (or at least keeping them at bay) could take as many as 17 minutes out of your week. And that's just not time you can spare, considering your rigorous napping schedule. Not to mention all the eating you have to get done.

One of the most realistic approaches to this problem is to learn how to just live with it. Embrace it. *Own* the dust and the dirt – after all, they're free – and how many other things in your house can you say that about?

Just be aware that people will inevitably talk. They'll judge you. Some, like your mother and your best friend, might even attempt an intervention. So it's good to have your defenses up. Here are some ready-made arguments for you to keep in your arsenal.

• Dirt boosts immunity: (This is a similar justification used by millions of new parents after accidentally dropping their baby's pacifiers on the ground.) Immune systems thrive on unseen bacteria, germs, and allergens. The more you let them build up around you, the stronger you get, and the less strain you put on this country's healthcare system. (And the less you have to interrupt your naps in order to go to the doctor.)

• Dust bunnies are endearing: Sure, they don't hop or wiggle their noses like the real one in your garden, but if you walk by them swiftly enough, the draft will cause them to roll end-over-end in an adorable way, just like baby tumbleweeds.

• Cobwebs are abstract art: The patterns they create are simultaneously complex yet simple. Modern art museums around the world pay big money for installations just like this.

• Dust mites make quiet pets: No barking, no meowing. You can't even hear them partying in your pillow all night when your ear is pressed right up against them.

• Dirty windows don't need curtains: Window treatments are a costly nuisance. If you let enough grime accumulate on the glass, it will provide all the privacy you need.

• Pig Pen is a hero: Charlie Brown's friend is perfectly comfortable with that swirl of dirt surrounding him, and for this reason, he is the epitome of self-acceptance. We could all use a little more of that — he's not disgusting, he's just different. Why be ashamed of dirt, when you could be proud?

# The Only Surefire Way to Get
# Your House Clean

You can wallow in your own mess and defend your dirt for a long time. But at a certain point, you are going to have to pull your house together. There is really only one way to this:

• Invite people over.

(Clarification: This is *not* so that they will help you clean, but is simply meant to serve as the ultimate motivational tool. Surely you don't want anyone to see the unhygienic depths to which you regularly sink.)

## The Do's and Don'ts of Being Neighborly

Oh, neighbors. Even if you live "in the middle of nowhere" there are still neighbors to contend with. They are by definition, the people who reside closest to you. Whether they live a few feet away or a few miles, these are guaranteed to be the most awkward relationships in your life. Sure, you may occasionally enjoy your neighbor's help and friendship and yet it is essential that you don't get *too* close. In sum, you don't really want them to know anything about you, but by the power of proximity, they know absolutely everything.

So you might as well make nice-nice with them and their pit-bull, too.

Here are some other guidelines to follow in order to help you cultivate this tricky relationship while also keeping them at arm's length:

• DON'T randomly look out your windows just in case your neighbors are looking out their windows at the exact same time. You don't want them to think you are stalking them. DO invest in a high-end telescope, turn off all your lights at night, and pretend that you're a budding stargazer with a bad sense of direction. (Oh! The stars are all the way up *there*?) How else are you supposed to find out whether your neighbors are running a meth lab out of their kitchen or merely experimenting with new cupcake recipes?

• DON'T try to one-up them with every purchase you make or project you undertake (i.e. shiny new car, snazzy moped, remodeled patio an acre wide). DO everything in your power to keep up with them if their last name happens to be Jones. If you are an American, this is one of your unalienable rights.

• DO ask them to watch your house when you go out of town. DON'T give them a key to your front door without first setting up hidden video surveillance to see if they're snooping through your medicine cabinet or your bureau drawers.

• DO agree to water their plants and feed their cats when they go out of town. DON'T forget about the video surveillance; after all they've probably read this guide, too. If you still have your heart set on snooping at their place, develop a disguise, an alibi, and tell them that you accidently left their keys (with their address written clearly on them) at the local public pool. (i.e. Wasn't me).

• DO compliment your neighbor's lawn. DON'T blow those fuzzy dandelion seeds in their direction (or don't let them see you doing it, anyway).

• DO give them a few brownies every time you bake a batch. DON'T ask them for a cup of sugar every time you undertake this baking project. (Maybe just keep it to every other time.)

• DO build a fence so that your dog, child, and stray badminton balls don't constantly invade their yard. As suggested previously, (see "Buying vs. Renting"),

DON'T build this fence even one millimeter over the property line, or without the help of a good surveyor, lawyer, mediator, boxing referee, and a poet by the name of Robert Frost (*"Good fences make good neighbors"…*)

• DON'T let your friends block your neighbor's driveway when you have a party. DO invite your neighbors to the party. After all, all those cars parked on the street are a dead give-away. And even if you have your friends bussed in from a discreet parking lot a few towns away, your neighbors will detect that you're having a party through the lens of their telescope, which, I hate to break it you, is far larger and more powerful than yours.

## How to Pick Reputable Repairpersons and other Service Personnel

The chances are high that, at some point, your dishwasher will break, your clothes dryer will stop working, and your furnace will go on strike. Chances are also high that these will all happen at the same time.

So how do you find people you can trust? The answer is that you really can't trust anyone, including yourself. All you can do is throw caution to the wind, cross your fingers, and remind yourself that a house is just an object, and it's not nearly as important as, say, your health. Although keep in mind that your health could be severely impacted by your house: for example, if you get electrocuted by live wires or get carbon monoxide poisoning from a clogged chimney. So, probably you should get a professional in, stat! Even an unprofessional professional is going to do better work than you would.

Here are some ways to go about finding someone:

• If you see a workman's (or workwoman's) van while you are out running errands, follow it with as much enthusiasm as personal injury lawyers are rumored to chase after ambulances.

• Throw darts at the yellow pages. Of course, nobody really uses the actual yellow pages these days – do they even exist anymore? If you find an old phonebook, most contractors in there have probably retired. But if you actually reach one, you'll probably sound so clueless and pathetic over the phone that he'll bust out his old toolbox for you, *pro bono*. Nothing inspires good workmanship more than pity.

• Do an exhaustive internet search of contractor listings. Then prepare a spreadsheet including how many stars they received in their customer ratings, their political affiliations, and their religious viewpoints. Once you have narrowed down the list, hire a private investigator to take care of the rest.

• Ask your friends who did the work they had done on their house. If you approve of the workmanship, there's no way of knowing if they will do equally good work for you. But if you *don't* actually like the workmanship, then voila – there's one less potential repairperson you can cross off your list. Don't ever underestimate the process of elimination.

• Hang out in the appropriate aisle of your local Home Depot or other gigantic home improvement superstore. For example, if your toilet is overflowing, head directly to the plumbing aisle. Professional plumbers are bound to come through looking for parts they need. No matter how busy they appear, or how much of a hurry they are in, sidle up into their personal space and say, "So, you come here often?"

## Keeping an Eye on Resale

Surely you have made a wise investment. Surely your neighborhood is going to become the next hottest place at some point in the next 30 years. (After all, *you* live there, that's definitely worth something - didn't local property values spike as soon as you moved in your decorative mushroom collection?) Surely you're going to be able to flip your place for a profit. Let's hope so, anyway, since that's the money with which you were planning to retire.

Here are some things to keep in mind:

• Don't hang any pictures, paintings or other artwork of any kind. This makes your walls as pocked and pitted as golf balls. Returning your walls to their smooth, original condition takes the precision and attention to detail that only a plastic surgeon can achieve. Then again, if you happen to *be* a plastic surgeon (or...plaster surgeon) or you are certain that you will be selling to one down the road, go crazy – hang it *all* up.

• Never *ever* burn a candle for religious, romantic, or practical reasons because it is very difficult to sell a house that is shaped like a pile of ashes.

• Brag about your house incessantly around town – you need to start creating a buzz and no amount of hyperbole is too much. Say things like, "Our house is just so big that I gave up my gym membership - I burn thousands of calories every time I jog from the screening room to the green house…" (i.e. from the TV to the plant in the corner). And: "Ever since George Washingtown slept here, I couldn't bring myself to wash his sheets." (i.e. a friend of a friend who was in town for a historical puppeteering conference, and you're just too lazy to clean up the guest room). How about: "No, I didn't get Botox, I simply spend two hours a day in our sauna." (i.e. ridiculously long and wasteful hot showers augmented with a heat lamp). Not only will be people be dying to buy your house, they'll be tripping over themselves to befriend you.

• Conversely, don't ever mention any of the "issues" you've had, such as your mouse infestation or the waist-high flood in your basement. If people ask about the tree they saw fall on your house, don't exactly deny it but don't confirm it either.

• Keep things extremely neutral. Don't even choose a beige or oatmeal palette. Go white, all the way. White walls, floors, cabinets, countertops, tiles, curtains, lamps, furniture, etc. That fake fruit in that ceramic bowl? Paint it white, too. This will create a blank slate for buyers, so that they can imagine their own color schemes and their own fake fruit arrangements. Besides, they will also temporarily think they have stumbled into heaven. (Especially if, for the open house, you hire a trio of monks to chant while wearing angel costumes. Highly recommended.)

• Finally, begin to study the ancient art of needlepoint so that you can craft a *Home Sweet Home* design to frame and display with pride (but not with nails, see above). Get started now, because it will take several years to master the highly dexterous needle and thread technique and to actually finish the project amid everything else you're trying to do. However, the final product will be worth it. It will quietly suggest to potential buyers the real truth…that despite (and because of) everything that has happened there, your house has been loved.

# Acknowledgments

I'd like to thank Rob for his support, his artwork (in these pages and elsewhere), and for taking such loving care of our plants. I'd also like to thank my sister-in-law, Bobbie Anne, for helping us buy our dream house, though it was the longest closing in history (or felt like it) and the course was filled with many obstacles. Finally, thank you to my parents for demonstrating what it is to be great homeowners, for real, and also for their good humor, respectively.